Usborne
Clothes
& Fashion
Picture Book

Ruth Brocklehurst

Illustrated by Christophe Lardot

Designed by Nancy Leschnikoff and Laura Wood

Fashion history consultant: Jemima Klenk

Contents

2	The first fashions	18	The Jazz Age
4	Age of magnificence	20	Hollywood glitz
6	Collars and cuffs	22	Fashion under fire
8	Wigs and panniers	24	New looks
10	Neoclassical style	26	Fashion goes pop
12	Corsets and crinolines	28	Directory of designers
14	Bustles and s-bends	30	Fashion timeline
16	Bicycles and bathers	32	Index

The first fashions

The very first trendsetters were the monarchs and rulers of ancient times, who dressed to impress in luxurious fabrics and fabulous jewels. Styles didn't change as quickly as they do today and were only followed by very wealthy people.

Egyptian pharaoh and his queen in tall crowns and ceremonial dress, around 3,350 years ago

Egyptian style

Ancient Egyptians, who lived between 2,000 and 4,000 years ago, took great care of their looks. They wore fine, pleated linen clothes with ornate collars and lots of jewels.

For special occasions, men and women wore wigs hung with beads. They made up their eyes with dark eyeliner, and painted their lips red.

Wall painting from an Ancient Egyptian tomb

A 3,330-year-old collar, or 'pectoral', shaped like a falcon

Greeks and Romans

The people of Ancient Greece and Rome wore loose, flowing clothes. These were made from simple rectangles of cloth that they draped around their bodies, and held in place with brooches and girdles.

Gold wreath crown, probably awarded for a special achievement, made around 2,400 years ago in Greece

Most Romans wore basic belted tunics. But for public events, high-ranking men wore 'togas' on top.

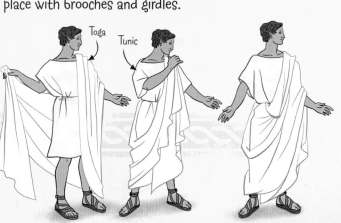

Toga

Tunic

I. To put on his toga, a man draped one end over his left shoulder.

II. Then, he brought the rest under his right arm.

III. Next, he threw the right end over his left shoulder.

IV. Then, he tucked the middle part into his belt.

Remains of Roman leather sandals from London, 1st or 2nd century

2

Byzantine opulence

Based in the magnificent city of Constantinople (now Istanbul), the Byzantine emperors and empresses of the 6th century imported cotton and linen from Egypt, furs from Europe and silk from China. Later, they brought back silk worms from China so they could produce their own silk cloth.

This mosaic shows the Byzantine Empress Theodora wearing an elaborate crown, set with jewels and hung with ropes of pearls.

Wealthy Byzantines wore lots of jewels, especially gold and pearls.

Hinged gold bracelet with pearls, amethysts, sapphires, quartz and emeralds, 1,500 years old

Gold earrings set with square-cut emeralds and amethysts

Pointed 'hennin' headdress with veil

Belted doublet

hose

Lords and ladies

In medieval Europe clothes became more fitted. Men wore jackets, or 'doublets', over leggings, or 'hose'. Women wore dresses with narrow waists and tight sleeves under sweeping gowns, and headdresses to cover their hair.

Richly patterned Italian silk velvet, like this piece from around 1450, was the most luxurious fabric of the age.

Pointed shoes known as 'pikes' or 'poulaines'

Fur-lined gown worn over a blue dress

This painting from the 1460s shows a fashionable lord and lady at their wedding.

Medieval headdresses

'Crispinette' headdress

Turban or 'chaperone' worn by men and women

Butterfly headdress

Heart-shaped headdress

Shoes like this were very fashionable in the 14th and 15th centuries. In 1463, King Edward IV of England passed a law that only men of high status were allowed to wear shoes with toes longer than 5cm (2inches).

Age of magnificence

Europe went through a 'Little Ice Age' in the 16th century, with temperatures much lower than today. Monarchs kept warm in sumptuous layers of velvet, silk, wool, furs and fine linen, all richly embroidered and encrusted with jewels. Meanwhile, a growing middle class of merchants and landowners did their best to keep up.

King Henry VIII of England painted by Hans Holbein in the most extravagant male fashion of the age, 1537

Kirtles and gowns

In the early 16th century, women's dress consisted of a gown, an undergown – known as a 'kirtle' – and a cone-shaped underskirt called a 'farthingale'.

Headdress edged with pearls

Black veil

Bodice with square neckline

Kirtle with close-fitting bodice

Sleeves with fur turn-ups

Girdle tied around the waist

False sleeves to match the kirtle

Gown

Kirtle

Waist ties

A farthingale had cane hoops sewn into it for support. This was worn with linen underwear, which was changed and washed frequently.

Outer clothes were made from thick, warm fabric. They were seldom washed, but dirt was brushed and beaten out of them, and the clothes were stored with bags of scented herbs to keep them fresh.

This jacket, from 1610, belonged to an English woman. You can see the embroidered design of scrolling vines, flowers and birds below.

Spanish style

From 1550, a new fashion spread from Spain: a pleated, lacy collar called a ruff. Soon, ruffs had grown so large that some had to be held up by wire frames.

'Cartwheel' ruff with figure eight pleats

Open ruff, mainly worn by unmarried women

Full lace ruff

Puffed sleeves

Stomacher

Wide, drum-shaped skirt

Cloak

Doublet

Bombasted breeches

Knitted hose

Dresses became wider too, supported by padding or hoops. At the front, women wore a stiffened panel, called a 'stomacher', which made them stand rigid and upright.

Embroidered stomacher, 16th century

Men added volume to their clothes too, by padding them with 'bombast' – rags, fleece, or even bran.

This is a detail from a 1588 portrait of Queen Elizabeth I of England. Many women copied her pale make-up and dyed their hair red or wore wigs.

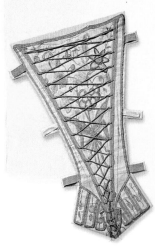

Fancy gloves were often given as gifts. This pair belonged to Queen Elizabeth I.

Platform shoes, or 'chopines' like these, were popular from 1580-1620. They were designed for women who didn't want to trail their skirts in muddy ground.

These necklaces are from the 'Cheapside hoard' – a box of jewels, hidden by a London goldsmith in his cellar in 1620 and discovered in 1912.

Gold and enamel

Garnet

5

Collars and cuffs

During the 17th century, fashion was led by the court of the French King Louis XIII – and Paris has been one of the world's fashion capitals ever since. Inspired by a passion for costly lace, courtiers wore white lace collars and frilly cuffs to match. But this was not a practical style for anyone doing manual work.

A lace collar and cuffs set, 1635

A nobleman's outfit, 1630s

'Baldric' sash for carrying a sword

Lace collar

Full sleeves cut into panels

High-waisted doublet

The Laughing Cavalier, painted by Frans Hals in 1624, shows a fashionable man wearing a particularly wide lace collar.

Knee breeches

Lace cuffs

Embroidered gauntlet gloves

From top to toe

Wide-brimmed hat with plume

Men's shoes decorated with ribbon or lace rosettes

'Bucket-top' boots with turnovers and lace trim

Spurs on the heels

Dating from the 1630s, this silk satin doublet and breeches would have belonged to a very wealthy man.

This close-up of the suit on the right shows the pattern, made by cutting tiny holes and stamping motifs into the cloth.

Stunning satin

In the 17th century, the most fashionable dresses were made from shiny satin, which had a more fluid drape than the heavy wool or velvet gowns of the previous century. They were usually worn with stiff corsets called 'stays'.

These stays have detachable sleeves, lace up the front for a perfect fit and are stiffened with thin strips of whalebone.

Silk dress fabrics, 1610s

This shade of carnation pink was especially popular during this period.

Tiered, elbow-length sleeves with lace cuffs

Lace handkerchief

Wide lace collar

Bodice with rosette detail at the waist

This woman's shoe is decorated with ribbon. All 17th-century shoes were 'straights', meaning they weren't shaped to fit the left or right foot.

A noblewoman's outfit, 1630s

At this time, children wore the same styles as their parents. But toddlers of both sexes were put in 'frocks' similar to the little boy's one in the middle.

The Three Eldest Children of Charles I of England, painted in 1635 by Anthony van Dyck

Simple styles

Strict Protestants, known as Puritans, disapproved of the fashion for bright satin and intricate lace. They preferred to dress in black with plain white collars and cuffs.

It was this costume that a group of Puritans, known as the Pilgrims, took with them to settle in America in 1620.

Wigs and panniers

A king with his own luxurious dress sense, Louis XIV of France imposed new styles on his followers. The lavish clothes of the French court – wigs and frock coats for men, and elegant silk dresses for women – dominated European fashion for most of the 18th century.

An engraving of Louis XIV, King of France from 1643-1715

Key looks for men

- ⚔ Knee-length leggings, called breeches, worn with stockings

- ⚔ Lace necktie called a 'jabot'

- ⚔ Knee-length frock coats, often with deep, turned-up cuffs and embroidered trim

- ⚔ Long waistcoat to match the coat

- ⚔ Heeled shoes with front buckles

- ⚔ Wide-brimmed hats, turned up on three sides, known as 'tricorn' hats

A long, embroidered man's waistcoat

In this close-up, you can see the silk and metal threads, and the sequins that adorn the waistcoat.

Elegant shoes like this, made from silk, were for indoor formal wear only.

Wigs and hairpieces

Wigs were the most distinctive fashion items of the day. Introduced by Louis XIV, soon most men were wearing wigs in public. The best wigs were made from human hair, but horsehair or wool was used for cheaper ones. Women often curled their hair with hot irons or added hairpieces. A few wore wigs.

Big wig, powdered white with starch, early 18th century

Small wig tied back with black ribbon, from 1730s

Lace cap with 'lappets' hanging at the back, 1740s

Powdered hair, piled high with hairpieces, 1760s

Wide dresses

Women's clothes were as sumptuous as the men's. Dresses had tight bodices and wide skirts, often made from floral silks adorned with ribbons, ruffles and lace.

Skirts were supported by oval hooped underskirts called panniers, from the French for 'baskets'. These were flat at the front and back, and wide at the sides.

Floral silk dress fabrics

This dress, from around 1760, is made from Chinese silk painted with flowers.

This dress would have been worn with a triangular insert called a stomacher. These were often beautifully embroidered.

Stays (shown here in red) stiffened with whalebone

Panniers

Some court dresses were so wide that women had to walk sideways to get through doorways.

Cotton chemise

Elbow-length sleeves with frilled cuffs

This 1779 portrait of Marie-Antoinette shows her wearing one of Rose Bertin's dresses.

Fashion and excess

During Louis XVI's reign women's hair styles and dresses were becoming even more elaborate. Queen Marie-Antoinette was renowned for her extravagant clothes, designed by Rose Bertin, her 'Minister for Fashion'.

Very few could afford such excessive fashions – but radical changes were on the way.

One of the more extreme hair styles, 1779

9

Neoclassical style

In 1789, revolution broke out in France, which led to great social changes throughout Europe, and new fashions too. Gone were the powdered wigs and flamboyant frills – the new look was all about simplicity, inspired by classical Greek and Roman statues.

Women pinned their hair in buns with soft curls at the sides.

High waisted 'Spencer' jacket worn over an empire-line dress

Bonnet

Paisley shawl

Small purse or 'reticule'

Parasol

Flat shoes or ankle boots

Decorative embroidery around the hem

Key looks for women

- ⚹ Empire-line (high-waisted) dresses in pale, gauzy fabric
- ⚹ Bonnets
- ⚹ Empire-line coats called 'pelisses' or 'Spencer' jackets
- ⚹ From the mid-1820s, waistlines become lower and skirts fuller.

Paisley pattern is based on an Indian or Middle Eastern design, but it is named after a Scottish town where wool shawls were made.

These ankle boots are typical of the period. The one to the left is made from kid leather; the one on the right is made of denim fabric.

Men's short, tousled 'Titus' haircuts were based on statues of the Roman Emperor Titus.

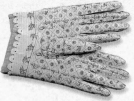

Gloves were always worn outside the house. This pair is made from printed leather.

Key looks for men

- ⚹ Plain blue tail coats worn over short waistcoats
- ⚹ Breeches tucked into riding boots
- ⚹ Cravats (a sort of necktie) knotted around high shirt collars
- ⚹ From around 1820, full-length trousers become fashionable instead of breeches.

This white tulle* netting evening dress, from around 1810, belonged to Empress Josephine of France.

The silver embroidered threads would have shimmered in the candlelight at balls.

Bonnets were essential wear for women outdoors, and could be decorated to match any outfit.

For evening wear, turban-style hats were popular.

Printed leather evening shoes with pom-poms on the toes, 1780-1800

Carved mother of pearl fan – perfect for keeping cool at a dance

Polished steel button from a man's jacket, 1810-1820

Male fashion was influenced by Beau Brummell (left) a friend of Britain's Prince Regent.

Oriental

Napoleon

Mail coach

Fashionable men, called 'dandies', had all kinds of different ways of tying their cravats.

* Tulle is fine net fabric named after the French city of Tulle.

Corsets and crinolines

By the middle of the 19th century, women's clothes had changed shape dramatically. Designed to create an hourglass figure, dresses looked demure and romantic, but they were also restrictive, uncomfortable and impractical.

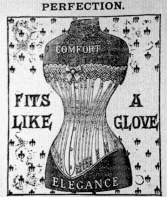

PERFECTION.

COMFORT

FITS LIKE A GLOVE

ELEGANCE

THOMSON'S "GLOVE-FITTING."
30 Years approval by the whole polite world. Of all drapers. Quality D 10s. 6d., E 8s. 6d., F 6s. 6d., G 4s.11d.
Ask for Thomson's "Glove Fitting," and take no other.
[9 c 19

An advertisement for a corset supposed to 'fit like a glove'

Modest style

Daytime dresses were usually made from printed wool or cotton. They were supposed to cover as much flesh as possible – it was considered vulgar for women to expose their ankles, even when walking.

Bonnet trimmed with silk flowers, 1845

Printed wool day dress, 1840s

Gathered bodice

Wide 'pagoda' sleeves

Floor-length bell-shaped skirt

Women cinched in their waists with tight corsets, and wore crinolines – stiff, heavy petticoats, hooped skirts or frames – to add volume to skirts.

Silk and whalebone corset, 1850s

1860s cage crinoline

An American named Amelia Bloomer campaigned for women to wear a tunic and pantaloons (often now called 'bloomers' after her) instead of restrictive undergarments. A few copied her, but most laughed at her.

Dressing up

For a ball or a night at the opera, women wore low-cut evening dresses. These were often made from silk or velvet adorned with ribbons and lots of jewels.

Pearl choker

Carnelian cameo necklace

Diamond drop earrings

Cameo brooch

Madame de Moitessier, (1844-1856) by Jean-Auguste-Dominique Ingres, is a portrait of a wealthy French woman in a fashionable evening dress.

Satin evening shoes, 1855-65

Sew easy

Until the invention of sewing machines in the mid-19th century, clothes were all sewn by hand.

Key looks for men

- Muted, dark shades
- Top hats worn by men of all social classes
- Small cravats
- Short waistcoats
- Long tailored jackets known as 'frock coats'
- Tartan or plaid in winter

Man's daytime outfit, 1850s

Pretty, printed floral dress fabrics like these were mass-produced and especially popular.

Embroidered patterned waistcoat, 1840s

Evening dress,
1884-86

Bustles and s-bends

From the 1870s, dress shapes changed from bell-shaped to being flatter at the front and fuller behind. This new silhouette was enhanced by flounces of fabric gathered at the back and supported using corsets and bustles.

Bustles – undergarments used to hold up full, heavy skirts at the back – stuck out, almost horizontally. They reached their most exaggerated proportions by the mid-1880s. Some were so large that people joked they could balance a tea tray on one.

Modified
crinoline,
1870s

Bustle pad
stuffed with
horsehair,
1875-80

Wire frame
bustle, 1880s

Wire frames were lighter than bustle pads, and provided better support for the heavy skirts.

The intricate folds and pleats of this dress are highlighted by the sheen of the silk satin.

Kid leather button-up boots, made in Vienna, 1895-1915

Men's casuals

Men's casual clothing became more varied. In town, a stylish man would wear a top hat or a bowler hat, a suit and a long jacket with contrasting collar. In the country, cream pinstriped suits were worn, usually with a boater.

The Bridesmaid, painted by James Jaques Tissot in 1883-85, shows a fashionable couple getting into a horse-drawn cab.

Bow tie

Man's
country
outfit, 1890s

Boater

Artistic alternatives

In artistic and intellectual circles, some began to reject the constrictive fashions of the day. Men dressed in smocks or lounge jackets while women wore loose gowns. They were influenced by a group of artists called the Pre-Raphaelite Brotherhood, whose work was inspired by medieval art and literature.

In this photograph from 1882, author Oscar Wilde wears 'aesthetic dress' – a velvet lounge jacket and breeches.

Liberty dress, 1900s

In 1875, Arthur Lasenby Liberty opened a shop in London, selling art and ornaments from India and the Far East. Liberty's fabric came to define the artistic styles of the time.

Liberty dress fabric, 1887

The Daydream, by Pre-Raphaelite artist Dante Gabriel Rossetti, 1880

Extreme curves

By the 1890s, bustles had gone out of vogue. Instead, the new fashionable silhouette was an exaggerated hourglass. It was achieved with a new style of corset that thrust the chest forward and the hips back. This was known as a straight front or 's-bend' corset.

C/B À LA SPIRITE

New Models LONG HIP All Shapes AT LEADING RETAILERS.

STRAIGHT FRONT CORSETS For The Woman of FASHION.

An advertisement for the new style of corset, 1903

Dresses clung to the hips, emphasizing the s-bend curve.

Bicycles and bathers

Known as the *Belle Époque*, or 'Beautiful Era', the early 20th century was a time of elegant, understated luxury. But fashions became more comfortable and practical too.

Linen day dress and matching hat, 1910

This Danish illustration from the early 1900s shows two young women wearing fashionable tailored skirt suits to ride their bicycles.

This outfit would have been perfect for a stylish garden party.

Key looks for women

★ Straight, ankle-length dresses with natural, often uncorseted, waists

★ Tailor-made suits for everyday wear

★ Art Nouveau-style accessories and details (see right)

★ Wide belts

★ Very wide-brimmed hats trimmed with flowers or lots of feathers

One-piece man's bathing suit

Bathing cap

Belted dress with sailor collar

Bloomers

Stockings and lace-up canvas bathing slippers

Bathing costumes were often made from taffeta or mohair, or even knitted, so they would have been very heavy when wet.

Sporting times

Many people enjoyed more leisure time than in earlier decades, and this was reflected in new clothing specially designed for different sporting activities such as cycling and swimming. Cycling was a relatively new passtime, and gave many women greater independence to get out and about.

Waved hair tied up in
a loose bun, 1905

Wide-brimmed hat, 1900-1914

Oriental-style turban, from 1912

Bone combs such as
this one were popular
for securing women's
hair styles.

A new opulence

During the early 1900s, fashion was
influenced by *Art Nouveau* – a style of
architecture and decorative art based on
curved lines and stylized plant forms.
Dress shapes became softer and more
fluid, and accessories more ornate.

This crocodile
skin handbag
from 1900 has a
swirling silver Art
Nouveau clasp and
corner decorations.

The 'Sorbet' dress,
designed by Paul
Poiret in 1912, was
partly inspired by the
drape of Japanese
kimonos.

Art Nouveau brooch, 1900

The world at war

In 1914, the First World War broke
out. As men were called up to fight,
women went to work in their place –
many for the first time. This meant
fashions became plainer and more
practical. Hard-wearing suits and
sensible shoes were the order of the
day, or sometimes even uniforms.

A British poster encouraging women to
join the Women's Royal Navy Service

The Jazz Age

During the 1920s, a new trendsetter emerged: the flapper girl. Young, free and single, she wore short dresses, cut her hair short and danced the night away in jazz clubs. Older generations disapproved, but the flappers' style soon caught on.

This is a 1921 fashion plate by French illustrator George Barbier. Hemlines varied a lot during the decade, from just above the ankles to just below the knees.

Feather headdress

Bow tie

Short hair, known as an 'Eton crop'

Low-waisted beaded dress

Dinner jacket

Evening dresses were adorned with sequins, beads and fringes to add sparkle and movement as women danced.

Pastel stockings

Dancing shoes with straps

Embroidered and beaded silk velvet evening dress with 'handkerchief' hem and tassels, 1923

Ostrich feather fans such as this added a dramatic touch to a flapper's outfit.

To go with shorter hair styles, long earrings became popular.

Gold leather shoes with printed flowers, 1925

Comfort and style

During the day, stylish women wore simple dresses with dropped waists or sporty suits made from draped wool jersey or tweed.

The new, straighter silhouette meant most women could exchange their corsets for simple slips and camisoles. But curvy women wore binding underwear to give themselves more boyish figures.

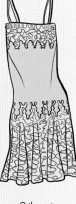

Silk and lace slip

Camisole trimmed with lace

Outdoors, women wrapped up in long coats, often trimmed with fur, like the one in this magazine advertisement from 1929.

The most popular style was a wrap-over that fastened at one side.

AINE - MONTAILLÉ
1, Place Vendôme — PARIS

Is now showing a winter collection

DRESSES
COATS
HATS
LINGERIE
PARFUMES

AIX-LES-BAINS - CANNES   NEW-YORK

Cloche hat

Following the flappers' tomboyish style, women of all ages had their hair cut short. During the day, they wore snug-fitting cloche hats (from the French for 'bell').

Straw cloche hat decorated with felt, ribbon and velvet appliqué, 1925

Women's day dresses, mid-1920s

Key looks for men

- Formal wear consisting of a tail coat over a waistcoat with a bow tie and top hat

- 'Dinner' jackets for informal evening events

- Sports wear including sweaters, caps and tweed 'knickerbockers'

"A woman needs ropes and ropes of pearls" Coco Chanel

Chanel

Gabrielle 'Coco' Chanel (left) was one of the most influential designers of the 20th century. Her simple, elegant designs defined the look of the 1920s. She revolutionized women's fashion with the launch of her 'little black dress'.

19

Hollywood glitz

The 1930s was a time of financial hardship for many people around the world. But in Hollywood, the movie industry boomed. Film stars became the fashion leaders of the age, and their fans pored over pictures in glossy magazines to find out what they were wearing both on-screen and off.

Cut of the cloth

Evening dresses became floor-length, figure-hugging and very elegant. They were often bias-cut – a style of dress made by cutting fabric with the weave facing diagonally, instead of straight, so that it clings to the body.

Plunging neckline

Fitted waist

Clutch purse

Shoulders and back left bare

Fur stole

Actress Bette Davis poses in a bias-cut satin evening dress.

Jean Patou evening dress, 1936

Diamond brooches to wear with an evening dress

For the first time in fashion history, dresses were designed to show off the shape of women's buttocks.

Glamorous day wear

Women's daytime suits and dresses were designed to create a tall, slim outline. They were close-fitting, and skirts often had pleats or a flare, so that they kicked out at the hem.

Narrow skirt falling to mid calf

Hat worn at an angle

Bow detail at the neck

Slim waist accentuated by a contrasting belt

Fabrics for day dresses were often printed with stylized flowers or graphic designs such as this.

Man's casual outfit

'Fedora' hat worn at an angle

Broad, padded shoulders

Wide lapels

Jacket with narrow waist

Wide legs

Sunbathing became fashionable in the 1930s. Women were eager to show off their tans in backless evening dresses and halterneck tops, as seen in this picture.

Finishing touches

The focus of 1930s fashion was the tailored fit of clothes. Accessories were kept simple but chic.

Following the example of their screen idols, many women began wearing make-up – especially powder and lipstick.

Crocodile skin box bag

Leather gloves

Lace-up shoes

Hats were worn for every occasion.

The lid of a 1930s powder compact

21

Fashion under fire

In 1939, the Second World War broke out. The fighting lasted for six years, and there were shortages of all kinds of goods, including clothes. But despite the hardships, people were determined to keep up their spirits and look their best.

This poster urges women to join the land army, taking on farming jobs left by men drafted to the armed forces.

Key looks for women

* Tailored, masculine-style jackets and coats with shoulder pads

* Narrow skirts – full skirts would waste fabric

* Nylon stockings (although they weren't always available)

* Slacks – practical for women taking on jobs left by men drafted to fight

* Sturdy, wedge-heeled shoes

Austerity chic

During the war, production of uniforms took priority over fashion. Out of uniform, fashions became more austere, and clothes were carefully designed to avoid wasting any fabric.

Square shoulders

Jacket with only four buttons

Blouson jacket

Slacks

Narrow skirt

Wedge-heeled shoes

Three outfits, based on designs produced for the British government's 'utility' range in 1942

Paris was occupied by the Germans, but the city's hatmakers kept working, making flamboyant designs, like these.

In case of air raids, people always carried gas masks with them. Most made do with simple canvas bags or boxes, but this unusually luxurious one is made from reptile skin.

Making do

Many essentials, including clothing, were rationed during the War and for some time after. People were given ration books with coupons to exchange for the equivalent of just one new outfit per year.

New buttons were rationed, so old ones were saved from worn out garments to be used again on new clothes.

Knitters would unravel old sweaters and reuse the yarn.

Governments produced posters encouraging people to 'make-do and mend'.

Special threads like these were made for mending stockings.

Nylon stockings were first introduced in the late 1930s, and usually had a seam at the back. They were often hard to come by, so some women took to painting their legs to look as though they were wearing stockings.

Headscarf fabric printed with patriotic slogans and wartime street signs, 1942

Hair care

Snood

Knotted headscarf

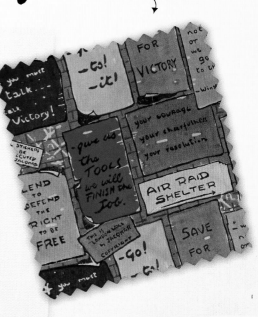

For special occasions, women used rollers to set waves into their hair, which they pinned up in rolls at the front.

The rest of the time, they often covered up with knotted headscarves or crocheted snoods, which kept hair safely out of the way for those working with machinery.

New looks

In 1947, Paris designer Christian Dior launched his first big collection, bringing a luxurious, romantic look back into fashion. After making do with practical clothes during the War, women were eager to adopt what became known as the 'New Look'.

This elegant outfit (left), known as the 'Bar Suit', defined the style of Dior's 1947 collection.

The New Look

- Rounded shoulders
- Nipped-in, often corseted, waists emphasized by belts or even padding on the hips
- Suits with fitted jackets
- Mid calf-length skirts
- Full-skirted evening dresses
- High-heeled shoes, gloves and hats

High fashion skirts were either very full or very narrow 'pencil' style.

Evening dresses fell just above the ankles, and were worn with net petticoats for extra volume.

Evening shoes were usually chosen to match a dress. They had slim 'stiletto' heels and pointed toes.

For formal occasions, women accessorized with big earrings. These are from New York designer, Tiffany & Co.

Fun in the sun

In the 1950s, many people had a lot more time and money to spend on leisure activities and sports. This gave rise to new fashions in casual, sporty clothing. Under American influence, beachwear including bikinis, Bermuda shorts and Hawaiian shirts became especially popular.

Sunglasses

Polka dot bikini

Hawaiian print shirt

Cotton day dress from Horrockses, London, 1955

Casual day dresses were usually made from cotton printed with fresh, bright floral patterns like this. Their narrow waists and full skirts were inspired by the New Look.

Actress Audrey Hepburn popularized the casual look of cropped 'capri' pants worn with ballet pumps.

Teenage kicks

For the first time, teenagers emerged as a distinct group with a style of their own. Instead of conforming to their parents' tastes, they danced to rock 'n' roll music and wore denim jeans* and circle skirts.

Denim jeans were first produced as work wear but the movie star James Dean (left) helped make them fashionable.

Slicked-back quiff

Girl's hair tied in a ponytail

Circle skirt

Denim jeans

'Saddle' shoes

Ankle socks

* The first jeans fabric was made in Italy in the Middle Ages. Weavers in Nîmes, France, then made their own, known as de Nîmes – 'from Nîmes' or denim.

Fashion goes pop

In the 1960s, fashions changed dramatically as trends were set in the streets of 'swinging' London. Led by daring designers and pop musicians, the new style was based on simple, clean shapes and bold shades. It was youthful, fresh and fun.

Fashion and art

Short shift dresses were fashionable, with a boyish silhouette similar to styles of the 1920s. But they were made from fabrics inspired by modern art – from Pop Art and geometric Op Art-inspired designs to swirling psychedelic patterns.

The miniskirt became popular, which drew attention to the legs. This led to a fashion for bright boots and tights.

Bold print by Emilio Pucci, 1968

Op Art print, 1966

London teenager Twiggy was one of the most famous models of the 1960s, and helped define the look of the period.

Key looks for women

- ↗ Miniskirts and shift dresses
- ↗ Bright, bold prints for dresses and shirts
- ↗ Tights, or pantyhose, in strong shades
- ↗ False eyelashes, black eyeliner and frosted lipstick
- ↗ Space Age clothes and accessories

Queen of the King's Road

In London, Carnaby Street and the King's Road attracted young shoppers looking for new, affordable designers. One of the most influential of these was Mary Quant (above) who is often credited with inventing the miniskirt.

Suede knee-high boots, Barbara Hulanicki, 1969

Advances in space science led to a craze for futuristic fashion made from shiny materials such as metal, leather and plastic.

Space Age sunglasses by Oliver Goldsmith, 1968

1960s hair styles

Flick

Beehive

'5-pointed bob' by London hairdresser Vidal Sassoon shown from the front and the side

Pillbox hat →

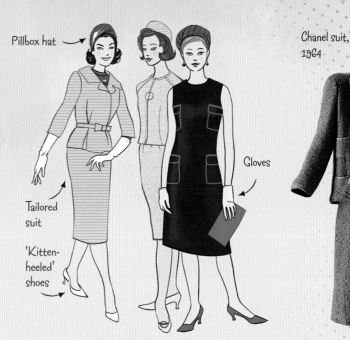

Tailored suit

'Kitten-heeled' shoes

← Gloves

Chanel suit, 1964

Grown-up style

Established designers incorporated elements of popular fashions, such as short skirts and shift dresses, into their collections. Worn by society women such as Jacqueline Kennedy, wife of the then US President, even tailored suits became less formal.

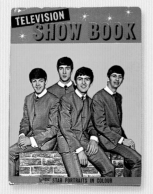

The Beatles, with their 'mop top' haircuts and collarless jackets, set the trend for young men in the early 1960s.

Peacock fashion

Previously, men's clothes had been fairly plain. From the 1960s, they started to wear slim suits and grow their hair. Later, in the so-called 'Peacock Revolution', dandies wore ruffled shirts, cravats, fur coats, velvet suits and vintage clothes. Men and women shopped at the same boutiques, so unisex styles became popular.

Royal Engineers jacket, 1914 teamed with 'loon pants', 1967

Hippies, 1968

Cheesecloth shirt →

Flares →

Maxi dress

Going with the flow

By the end of the decade, the sharp look of the early 1960s was giving way to something freer. Maxi dresses, kaftans, flares and striped 'loon pants' were all the rage, and black people grew big, bouncy 'Afro' hair-dos.

Directory of designers

Leading designers have set fashions since the late 19th century. They put on shows to launch each new range of clothing, and their styles are then adapted for the mass market. Here are some of the most influential:

1970s gold lurex halterneck dress

Giorgio Armani

Dates: 1934-present
Nationality: Italian

Especially noted for his relaxed, minimal style, Armani makes elegant, uncluttered day wear for men and women.

Cristóbal Balenciaga

Dates: 1895-1972
Nationality: Spanish-born; based in Paris

Renowned for the innovative shapes of his women's wear in the 1950s and 60s, including 'cocoon' coat and 'sack' dress.

A model poses in a Balenciaga coat, 1950

Coco Chanel

Dates: 1883-1971
Nationality: French

Credited with inventing the 'little black dress', Chanel defined 1920s style. She made simple, classic women's wear, often in jersey fabric.

André Courrèges

Dates: 1923-present
Nationality: French

Trained as a civil engineer before becoming a designer. Famous for making geometric shaped dresses in the 1960s, often with cut-out panels and Space Age accessories.

Christian Dior

Date: 1905-1957
Nationality: French

Classic haute couture ('superior dressmaking' in French) designer who introduced the 'New Look' in 1947.

Roy Halston

Dates: 1932-1990
Nationality: American

Designer of slinky dresses and jumpsuits, often halterneck or one-shouldered, that were popular in exclusive discos in the 1970s.

Calvin Klein

Dates: 1942-present
Nationality: American

Designer of simple, sophisticated casual clothing, denim and underwear.

Advertisement for one of Lanvin's mother and daughter outfits, 1920

Pierre Cardin

Dates: 1922-present
Nationality: Italian-born French

Studied architecture before going into fashion. In the 1960s, his designs featured geometric motifs and were inspired by the Space Age.

1960s Space Age outfit

Jean-Paul Gaultier

Dates: 1952-present
Nationality: French

Brought kilts and skirts into fashion for men, and introduced corsets as outerwear for women.

Early 1990s corset and kilt

Jeanne Lanvin

Dates: 1867-1946
Nationality: French

Designer who created romantic dresses, and mother and daughter outfits.

Ralph Lauren

Dates: 1939-present
Nationality: American

Studied business in New York before becoming a designer, rising to fame in the 1970s. Specializes in tailored clothes, inspired by vintage clothing.

Alexander McQueen

Dates: 1969-2010
Nationality: British

Celebrated for his theatrical style and precise tailoring.

Issey Miyake

Dates: 1938-present
Nationality: Japanese

Best-known for his sculptural dress shapes and pleated fabrics.

Mid-1990s
pleated dress

Jean Patou

Dates: 1880-1936
Nationality: French

Famous for his simple, streamlined designs during the 1920s. He dressed sports stars and actresses.

Jean Patou dress
design, 1925

Paul Poiret

Dates: 1879-1944
Nationality: French

Made his name in the 1910s designing flamboyant, oriental-inspired draped dresses and coats.

Mary Quant

Dates: 1934-present
Nationality: British

Rose to fame in the 1960s, when her miniskirts and bright shift dresses appealed to young fashion followers.

Paco Rabanne

Dates: 1934-present
Nationality: Spanish

Caused a stir in the 1960s with his use of metals, paper, leather and plastic in his futuristic dress designs.

Yves Saint Laurent

Dates: 1936-2008
Nationality: French, born in Algeria

His women's wear was often influenced by masculine tailoring. In 1966, he became one of the first to make 'ready to wear' clothes in standard sizes.

Elsa Schiaparelli

Dates: 1890-1973
Nationality: Italian

Designed and sold knitwear before becoming a dressmaker in the 1920s. Noted for her witty, eccentric designs, and for working with surrealist artists.

Valentino

Dates: 1932-present
Nationality: Italian

Valentino Garavani's romantic evening dresses are popular among film stars and royalty.

Vionnet bias-cut
evening dress,
1932-34

Gianni Versace

Dates: 1946-1997
Nationality: Italian

Started out working with his mother, a dressmaker, before setting up his own company. Made elegant, tailored clothes.

Madeleine Vionnet

Date: 1876-1975
Nationality: French

Parisian dressmaker who introduced the bias-cut method in the late 1920s for making sleek, figure-skimming dresses.

Vivienne Westwood

Dates: 1941-present
Nationality: British

Opened a shop in London selling outrageous punk clothes in the 1970s. Her designs focus on tailoring and often give a modern twist to outfits inspired by fashions of the past.

Charles Frederick Worth

Dates: 1825-1895
Nationality: British; based in Paris

Worth was one of the first fashion designers to produce seasonal collections to show to his customers. He popularized the bustle in the 1870s.

Worth evening dress
with bustle, 1872

Fashion timeline

4,000 years ago
Ancient Egyptians wear pleated linen and beaded collars.

3,500 years ago
Ancient Greeks dress in loose clothes, draped around their bodies and fastened with brooches.

2,000 years ago
Important Romans wear shawls called togas over simple tunics.

1830s–1860s
Women's dresses become full and bell-shaped, worn over tight corsets and crinolines. Top hats are worn by men of all classes.

1790s–1820s
Inspired by ancient Greek and Roman statues, women wear 'empire-line' dresses. Fashionable men wear understated suits and knotted cravats.

1774–1792
The Queen of France, Marie Antoinette leads women's styles.

1873
Levi Strauss patents denim jeans.

1875
Liberty opens in London.

1870s–1890s
Women's dresses become flat at the front and full and flouncy at the back, supported by bustles.

1848
Isaac Singer patents the sewing machine.

1939–45
The Second World War breaks out. Rationing leads to 'austerity' fashions as people cope with shortages of fabric and clothing.

This woman is having her legs painted with fake stocking seams.

1930s
Hollywood movie stars influence new glamorous styles. The fashionable silhouette is sleek and fitted.

1947
Christian Dior launches the 'New Look'.

1950s
Teenagers emerge as a new group of consumers with their own fashions inspired by rock 'n' roll music.

1955
Mary Quant, often credited with inventing the miniskirt, opens her first shop on London's King's Road.

1960s
Fashion is influenced by the youthful styles worn in 'Swinging London'.

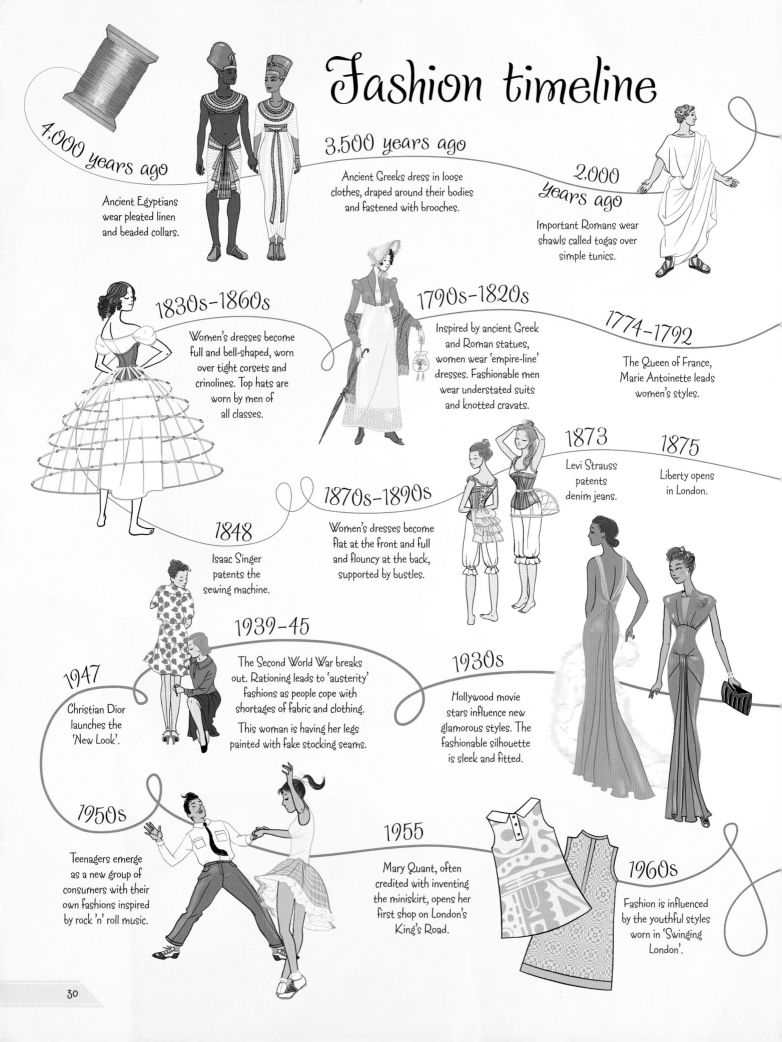

500s
Wealthy Byzantines dress in richly patterned silk robes and lots of jewels.

1200s–1400s
Medieval men wear doublets and hose with long, pointed shoes. The women wear flowing gowns and elaborate headdresses.

1500s–1550s
Kings, queens and their courtiers dress to impress in layers of wool, silk and velvet, embroidered and encrusted with jewels.

1690s
King Louis XIV of France starts wearing powdered wigs. They remain in fashion for much of the 18th century.

1630s
Under the influence of the French royal court, wide lace collars and matching cuffs become fashionable.

1550s–1600s
A Spanish fashion for lace ruffs spreads throughout Europe.

1880s–1900s
Casual dress for men includes sporty suits and straw boaters.

1890s
The s-bend silhouette is fashionable for women.

1900s–1910s
Increased popularity of sports, including cycling and swimming, leads to new styles of sports wear.

1909
Gabrielle 'Coco' Chanel sets up her first shop in Paris.

1920s
Flappers set the trends for women, and hemlines rise to knee-length for the first time.

1914–1918
The First World War breaks out. Many women go into uniform as they join auxiliary services to support the war effort.

1961–1963
As the wife of the US President, Jacqueline Kennedy defines the more grown-up, 'couture', look of the 1960s.

1968
Hippies get together at music festivals during the so-called 'Summer of Love'. They wear flares, kaftans and flowers in their hair.

1970s–present
Fashions become increasingly diverse as designers take inspiration from a wide range of influences, including styles of the past, and from around the world.

Index

A

accessories, 16, 17, 21, 26, 28
art, 26
Art Nouveau, 16, 17

B

bags, 17, 21, 22
bathing costumes, 16, 25
Belle Époque, 16
Bertin, Rose, 9, 30
bias-cut, 20, 29
bodices, 4, 7, 9, 12
bow ties, 14, 18, 19
breeches, 5, 6, 8, 10, 15
brooches, 2, 13, 17, 20, 30
bustles, 14-15, 29, 30
Byzantine, 3, 31

C

Chanel, Coco, 19, 28, 31
children, 7
coats, 8, 10, 19, 27, 28, 29
collars, 2, 5, 6-7, 10, 16, 30, 31
corsets, 7, 12-13, 14, 15, 19, 28, 30
  s-bend, 14-15, 31
cotton, 3, 11, 12, 25
cravats, 10, 11, 13, 27, 30
crinolines, 12-13, 14, 30
crowns, 2, 3
cuffs, 6-7, 8, 9, 31

D

dandies, 11, 27
denim, 10, 25, 28, 30
designers, 17, 19, 24, 26, 27, 28-29
Dior, Christian, 24, 30
doublets, 3, 5, 6, 31
dresses, 3, 4, 5, 6, 7, 8, 9, 10, 11, 12, 13, 14, 15, 16, 17, 18, 19, 20, 21, 24, 25, 26, 27, 28, 29
empire-line, 10, 30
evening, 11, 13, 14, 18, 20, 24, 29
shift, 26, 27, 29

E

earrings, 3, 13, 18, 24
Egypt, ancient, 2, 3, 30
embroidery, 4, 8, 9, 10, 11, 13, 18

F

fans, 11, 18
farthingales, 4
First World War, 17, 31
flappers, 18, 31
flares, 27, 31
France, 6, 8, 9, 10, 11, 18, 19, 28, 29, 30, 31
fur, 3, 4, 19, 20, 27

G

gloves, 5, 6, 10, 21, 24
Greece, ancient, 2, 10, 30

H

hair styles, 9, 10, 17, 18, 23, 27
hats, 6, 8, 11, 16, 17, 19, 21, 22, 27, 28
  boaters, 14, 31
  bonnets, 10, 11, 12
  bowler hats, 14
  cloche, 19
  fedoras, 21
  pillbox, 27
  top hats, 13, 14, 19, 30
haute couture, 28
headdresses, 3, 4, 18, 31
Hollywood, 20-21
hose, 3, 5, 31

J

jackets, 3, 4, 10, 13, 14, 15, 18, 19, 21, 22, 24
Jazz Age, 18

jeans, 25, 30
jewels, 2, 3, 4, 5, 13, 18, 31

K

Kennedy, Jacqueline, 27, 31
kirtles, 4

L

lace, 2, 5, 6, 7, 8, 9, 19, 31
leather, 10, 11, 14, 18, 21, 26, 29
Liberty, 15, 30
linen, 2, 3, 4, 16, 30
Louis XIV, King, 8, 31

M

make-up, 2, 5, 21
Marie-Antoinette, Queen, 9, 30

N

New Look, 24-25, 28, 30

P

paisley patterns, 10
panniers, 8-9
petticoats, 12, 24
plastic, 26, 29
Poiret, Paul, 17, 29
Pre-Raphaelite Brotherhood, 15

Q

Quant, Mary, 26, 29, 30

R

Rome, ancient, 2, 10, 30
ruffs, 5, 31

S

satin, 6, 7, 13, 14, 20
Second World War, 22 - 23, 24, 30

sewing machines, 13, 30
shirts, 25, 26, 27
shoes, 3, 5, 6, 7, 8, 10, 11, 13, 17, 18, 21, 22, 24, 25, 27, 31
  ballet pumps, 25
  boots, 6, 10, 14, 26
  platform shoes, 5
  sandals, 2
silhouettes, 14, 15, 19, 31
silk, 3, 4, 6, 8, 9, 11, 12, 13, 14, 19, 31
skirts, 5, 9, 12, 14, 22, 24, 25, 26, 27, 28, 29, 30
  miniskirts, 26, 27, 29
sleeves, 3, 4, 5, 6, 7, 9, 12
sportswear, 16, 19, 25, 31
stays, 7, 9
stockings, 8, 16, 18, 22, 23, 30
stomachers, 5, 9
suits, 6, 14, 16, 17, 19, 21, 24, 27, 31
sunbathing, 21

T

togas, 2, 30
trousers, 10, 22
tunics, 2, 12, 30
turbans, 11, 17

U

underskirts, 4, 9
  (see also farthingale, kirtle)
underwear, 4, 9, 12, 14, 19, 28
uniforms, 17, 22, 31

V

velvet, 3, 4, 7, 13, 15, 18, 31

W

waistcoats, 8, 10, 13, 19
weddings, 3
wigs, 2, 5, 8, 31
wool, 3, 4, 7, 12, 3